Fujisawa Healthcare, Inc.

Under My Skin

A Kid's Guide to Atopic Dermatitis

By Karen Crowe

Illustrated by Norm Bendell

Table of Contents

Dear Reader,

You know better than anyone: atopic dermatitis can really get *under your skin!* Rough, red patches and fingernail scratches may make you want to hide. Treatments can take lots of time and be messy. And your skin may itch so much at times you can hardly stand it! All this can make you feel frustrated and alone.

But did you know that millions of people around the world have atopic dermatitis? In fact, about one out of five kids are affected by it at some time! You'll meet a number of them throughout this book. They've shared their experiences and advice for dealing with atopic dermatitis, hoping to make coping with it easier for you.

Unfortunately, there's no cure for this skin disease; it's a continuing problem unless you're lucky enough to outgrow it. But good skin care can help you keep your itch and rash under control. This book will explain what's going on *under your skin* that causes it to flare. You'll learn ways to prevent itching and how to treat rashes when they occur. You'll also find pages to fill out that will help you manage your skin better.

We hope this book will answer your questions and help bring your skin relief. Ignoring atopic dermatitis won't make it go away. Taking control of your treatment really helps. So read on to find out what you can do to start improving your skin's condition today!

Your Friends at Fujisawa Healthcare

"I have to get up extra early to take a bath and moisturize before I go to school. Kids tease me because of my eczema. It bothers me because I don't want to be different."

Jeffrey J.
Age 9, Michigan

 "The worst thing about having eczema is when there are parties at school. I can't eat food I really like— like cupcakes and ice cream— or my skin will be itchy and hurt."

Sydney J.
Age 8, New Jersey

 "I don't want people to see the spots on my knees and elbows. It's embarrassing. I wish I could just forget about my skin and not have to take care of it all the time!"

Marquise L.
Age 8, Florida

 "I can't go out in the middle of the afternoon when it's hottest because sweat makes me itch. I get very upset because that's when all my friends are out playing."

Christopher D.
Age 9, Florida

Here are some of the problems that kids with atopic dermatitis are dealing with.

 "At sleepovers I don't want to put skin cream on. I don't like to go to school with ointment showing around my mouth, but if I don't, it gets so dry it sometimes bleeds or looks all chapped."

Amy R.
Age 11, Connecticut

 "I can't go swimming in pools because of my eczema. It makes me sad— I just sit on the side and watch."

Cherisse C.
Age 7, Florida

 "Some years, I've worn pants all the time—even during the summer— because my skin looked so bad."

Delynn S.
Age 11, Georgia

 "I itch all the time. It makes me crazy! I scratch all night long. I even scratch in my sleep. I wake up every night!"

Rachel P.
Age 5, Florida

The Physical Side

There's no denying you have atopic dermatitis—
you can **see** it with your eyes and **feel** that awful itch!
This section is all about what's happening inside your
body to **cause** the things you see and feel.

What Is Atopic Dermatitis?

AD Basics

Atopic dermatitis (ay-TOP-ic der-ma-TY-tus), also known as *eczema* (ECK-ze-muh) or "AD," is a disease that causes skin to be very dry and extremely itchy. The urge to scratch may be so uncontrollable that people scratch their skin until it bleeds. Once the skin is broken open, it may become infected.

AD rashes come and go. They may get worse or better during certain seasons, or even during the course of a day. At night, the itching may be so bad that it keeps people from sleeping. Most kids with AD have had it since they were infants, but the skin condition can also develop when kids are older.

The Looks of It

Atopic dermatitis may look different on every person. It often occurs in the bend of the elbows and behind the knees, but it's also found on the hands, feet, arms, legs, trunk of the body, scalp, face, and/or behind the ears—it can even cover the entire body in severe cases.

People with AD often have patches of skin that are scaly and inflamed (red and swollen). Your skin may be thickened (raised and tough) and discolored (red to brownish-gray) due to long-term scratching or rubbing. It may also be cracked or flaky, have scabs, or have lost its color altogether. If areas of skin become infected, they may have little fluid-filled bumps that ooze or become covered with yellow crust.

The Way It Feels

Maybe even more upsetting to you than the way AD looks is the way it feels: unbearable itching, painful blisters, raw, peeling skin. The skin at your joints may even be stiff and difficult to bend. Dealing with these discomforts can make a person very cranky. It's OK to hate having AD—most kids do! But don't let your anger keep you down. (Pages 27-36 will give you tips for dealing with the sadness or frustration you may be feeling.)

Why Do I Have AD?

Your atopic dermatitis is probably caused by a combination of things. Doctors are still studying this skin disease to find out more about it. These pages explain what *is* known about your awful itching.

The Reason for Your Rashes

The exact cause of eczema is not known, but doctors think it's a type of allergy that's passed down through families. If one of your parents has had AD, there's a 60% chance you'll have it, too. If both your parents have had eczema, there's an 80% chance you'll be itching along with them. In addition, if one of your parents has had asthma or hay fever, your chances of having AD also increase.

What causes your AD to flare up, or get worse? Just as with other kinds of allergies, there may be things about your environment (your surroundings at home, school, or any other place you spend time) that can make your itching and rash worse. Also, your lifestyle (the way you do certain things) can cause flare-ups. The things that make your AD flare are called triggers. (Pages 11-25 explain triggers in more detail.)

The Truth of the Matter

One thing is certain: it's no one's fault that you have eczema. Nothing you or your parents did or didn't do caused you to get AD. You're not unclean or overly emotional, and it's not the result of poor nutrition, as some people who don't know any better might guess. And eczema is not contagious—you can't "give" it to anyone else.

The Itch That Rashes

AD is often called the "itch that rashes." That's because your skin usually starts to itch before a rash appears. It's not until after you scratch your skin that the rash develops. The more you scratch, the worse the rash becomes. To find out what's happening in your body that makes you want to scratch, turn the page.

What Causes Skin to Itch?

Understanding *why* your skin itches can give you more control over your disease—and help you keep your AD from getting worse!

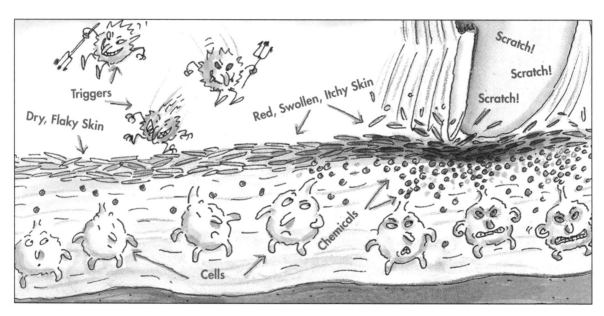

When people are exposed to triggers—things that their skin or bodies are sensitive to—certain cells in their skin release natural chemicals in defense. These chemicals act as a kind of barrier to protect the skin from whatever is "invading" the body.

Unfortunately, these chemicals also cause itching, redness, and swelling. The chemicals go away after a short time in people *without* AD. But in people who have AD, the cells don't switch off as they should—instead, the cells keep producing chemicals, so the itching continues.

The problem gets worse when you scratch or rub the itchy area. Scratching further aggravates your skin and causes the cells to release more chemicals, which make you itch and scratch even more. This is called the itch-scratch cycle. It's a frustrating cycle that's tough to stop!

Common Triggers

In this chapter, you'll learn all about **triggers**—the things that cause your skin to **flare.** The key to controlling your AD is to avoid the things your skin is **sensitive** to. So turn the page to get the facts about triggers—and learn how to ditch your **itch!**

That Darned Dry Skin

Most AD flares happen when people bathe or moisturize incorrectly. Read on to learn how you can avoid common mistakes.

Why Dry Is Dreadful

The skin's main job is to protect the body by keeping things on the outside—like dirt, germs, and chemicals—from harming things on the inside. In order for skin to work right, though, it needs to be flexible, which means it has to stay moist.

But people with AD have a defect in their skin that keeps it from staying moist. When their top layer of skin gets dry, it becomes brittle and it may crack. Then things outside the body can get inside, irritating skin layers below and triggering a rash.

Moisture Mania!

The best way to prevent skin from drying is to apply moisturizers often. To keep your skin healthy, use rich creams or ointments that your doctor recommends, not lotions, which contain a lot of water or alcohol and can actually dry the skin. Apply moisturizers throughout the day, whenever your skin feels dry, as well as right after bathing.

Better Bathing

Baths and/or showers are usually very helpful in treating AD. They add moisture to the skin and rid rash areas of germs and other things that can be irritating. The key is to moisturize immediately after getting out of the water. If you don't, your skin will become drier, making your eczema worse.

As soon as you finish bathing, gently pat your skin with a towel, leaving the skin a little damp. Then smooth on a thick coating of moisturizer to seal in water that's left on your skin. Here are some other bathing rules to follow to keep skin moist.

- Don't use soap unless dirt won't come off with plain water. (Soap removes the natural oils on your skin that help it stay moist.) Instead, use a mild moisturizing skin cleanser, and don't lather all over—just wash the places where it's needed, then rinse well.

- Use warm or cool water for bathing, not hot. Hot water evaporates quickly off skin, causing it to dry out.

- Avoid bubble baths, bath oils, and scented bath salts, which can aggravate AD.

- Keep baths and showers short— 5 to 10 minutes is enough. Any longer and your body's natural oils begin to get washed away.

- Don't rub your skin with a washcloth—it will irritate your skin.

- Use a mild shampoo, and wash your hair in a sink or shower instead of in the tub. That way, the lather won't linger on your skin.

- Your doctor may suggest soaking with medicated oatmeal bath powder. This can help soothe itching.

Turn to page 44 and jot down any questions you have for your doctor, as well as notes about bathing or moisturizing that you want to remember.

Those Irritating Irritants

What Are Irritants?

Irritants are things that come in contact with your skin and cause it to itch, burn, dry out, or turn red. These reactions usually happen very quickly after the irritant contacts your skin.

Common Irritants

- wool and other rough fabrics
- laundry detergents and drier sheets
- anything with fragrance, including perfumes, colognes, deodorants, and lotions
- some cosmetics and skin care products
- tobacco smoke ∎ paint ∎ chlorine
- cleaning products ∎ acidic foods

What You Can Do

- Don't wear wool—the sharp fibers irritate skin. Watch for other places you might come into contact with wool besides your own clothing: don't use a wool blanket on your bed, don't snuggle up to anyone wearing a wool sweater, and don't lie down on a wool carpet to watch TV.

- Avoid clothes made from other itchy or stiff fabrics such as polyester, nylon, or acrylic. Instead, wear soft, loose-fitting cotton clothes.
- Remove clothing tags that rub against the skin. Also avoid clothes with rough seams or trim.

- Wash new clothes before wearing to soften and to remove any chemicals on the fabric.
- Use a dye-free and perfume-free clothes detergent, and rinse laundry twice to remove any soap left behind.
- If your feet are flaring, give them a break— wear shoes no more than necessary. Try to buy shoes made of leather or some other material that breathes— *not* nylon or plastic.

"My feet get itchy when they're hot and sweaty. I wear sandals whenever I can to keep my feet cool."

Patrick O.

Age 6, Florida

- Avoid eating or preparing acidic foods (such as tomatoes or citrus fruits) if they seem to trigger a rash.
- Wear rubber gloves any time you use cleaning products. (Latex-free gloves with a lining are best.)
- Avoid breathing paint fumes and smoke.

Turn to page 45 to record your notes about irritants.

Ahh... Ahh... Allergens!

What Are Allergens?

Sometimes kids with AD notice that their skin gets worse when they're exposed to allergens—things they're allergic to, which their bodies try to fight. Everyone with AD should stay away from the irritants listed on pages 14 and 15, but you only need to avoid allergens if you're allergic. Avoiding allergens will help your skin itch less *and* soothe your runny nose and watery eyes, too.

Common Allergens

- pet dander
- pollen
- dust mites
- mold
- certain foods

What You Can Do

- If you're allergic to a pet, the best solution is to have a neighbor or nearby relative adopt your furry friend. But if you can't bear to part with a pet, vacuum your house often and keep your pet off your bed and other furniture you use— or outside.

- If you're allergic to pollen, stay inside as much as you can during allergy season. Keep windows closed— use a fan or air conditioner to keep cool instead. When you *do* go outside, avoid playing on the grass, and bathe before going to bed to rinse off any pollen that is clinging to your skin or hair.

- If you're allergic to dust mites, buy special covers for your mattress and pillow. Remove carpets and curtains from your bedroom if possible— if not, clean them often. Also wash your bed sheets and comforter frequently in hot water. Stuffed animals are dust-catchers, too, so if you can't give them up, give them a hot bath now and then.

- Mold grows in damp, dark places. If you're allergic to it, avoid basements, and keep the shades up in your bedroom to prevent it from growing, especially if you use a humidifier.

- Don't eat foods that seem to trigger flare-ups or make your rash worse. The foods kids are most commonly allergic to include: milk, eggs, nuts, wheat, soy, and seafood. (To make sure your diet stays balanced, check with your doctor before eliminating any foods.)

"I can't eat anything made with milk. But we found special vanilla soy ice-cream sandwiches at a store, and they're great!"

DUSTIN H.
Age 6, Iowa

Turn to page 45 to write down details about any allergies you have.

Don't Sweat It!

The Trouble with Temperatures

Kids with AD have very sensitive skin. Sometimes flare-ups occur when the temperature changes suddenly—such as when you step indoors to warm up after playing out in the snow, or when you leave a cool air-conditioned store on a hot summer day.

Hot and cold weather may trigger your AD in other ways, too. During cold winter months, the heat indoors can make your skin even drier and itchier than normal. (The hot, dry air causes moisture everywhere to evaporate, including moisture in your skin.) On humid summer days, increased sweat can irritate your skin and cause your AD to flare.

"Since sweat makes me itch, I try to wear light-colored clothing to keep from getting hot."

Age 12, Illinois

Solutions for All Seasons

Here are some suggestions to help you keep comfy year round:

■ Try to stay indoors during very hot or very cold weather whenever possible.

■ If sweat irritates your skin, avoid vigorous exercise, especially when your skin is flaring. If you are active, wear cotton clothing (it "breathes," so you'll perspire less and sweat will evaporate easily). Also, bathe as soon as you can afterwards to wash off sweat.

■ Ask your doctor to recommend a good sunscreen. Some gels are drying.

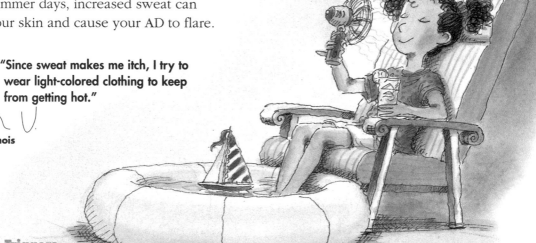

- Wear layers of clothing during all seasons so you can remove items when you feel too warm.
- Lower the temperature in your bedroom at night, and wear lighter pajamas to bed to prevent sweating while sleeping.
- Keep your skin warm in winter by covering it when you go outside.

- During winter months, use a cool-mist humidifier to help keep the air in your bedroom moist. (If you're allergic to mold or dust mites, be careful—they both like humidity. Clean your humidifier daily to prevent mold from growing, and follow the suggestions on page 17 to guard against dust mites.)
- The best way to prevent "winter itch" is to moisturize regularly. You can also use lip balm to help keep lips from becoming chapped.

Turn to page 45 and list ideas for keeping skin healthy in all kinds of weather.

Stressing Out?

Emotions That Trigger

Many kids with AD notice that stressful times or events make their eczema worse. Stress includes feelings of frustration, worry, embarrassment, anger, and even extreme tiredness. These emotional states can all cause your skin to "flush" or blush. When this happens, extra blood surges through your skin, especially in your face, causing it to redden. For kids with AD, this increased activity in the skin may cause itching.

Spot the Problems

Some things that may make you emotional include fights with family members, a friend moving away, or a big game coming up. School struggles such as test-taking, being called on in class, or homework overload may also make you feel stressed. And AD itself—and your treatment routine—can be a cause of frustration, too.

Sometimes you can learn to recognize and avoid the situations that bother you. When stressful things can't be avoided, though, try to cope with your feelings in other ways. Discuss what upsets you with a parent, friend, or your doctor. They may be able to suggest ways to help lower your stress. The tips on the right and the calendar on page 36 can also help you deal with stress.

Sports are a great way to reduce stress. Just don't let close calls or other tense moments take the fun out of your games!

Stress-Busters

Try these calming tips to prevent getting tense:

- Organize your time. Plan ahead so you don't feel rushed getting ready in the morning, studying for tests, or completing school projects.

- Take breaks during study sessions. Walk around, breathe deeply, get a drink of water, or stretch to relax your muscles and energize your mind.

- Exercise regularly— *if* sweat isn't a problem for you. A half-hour of activity three times a week will help your body flush out unhealthy chemicals that build up in your blood due to stress.

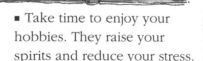

- Take time to enjoy your hobbies. They raise your spirits and reduce your stress.
- Celebrate small successes you achieve each day, such as going scratchless or getting a good grade. (Pages 27-36 give more ideas for keeping a positive outlook.)

Turn to page 46 to record notes about stress.

De-stressing Tips

Here are some soothing suggestions from kids.

"I scratch when I'm very nervous—like when school was just starting or when I go on amusement park rides. To relax, I take a breath and slowly count to ten. I keep doing this until I feel better."

Maxine M.
Age 6, Florida

"We go on morning and night walks. It takes my mind off my itching, makes me feel stronger, and helps me calm down and get sleepy."

Nayha R.
Age 7, Massachusetts

"My skin gets itchy when I'm nervous. Playing with my Gameboy helps me relax and keeps me from scratching."

Patrick O.
Age 6, Florida

All about Infections

Why Do They Happen?

Kids with AD get skin infections more easily than kids with normal skin. Here's one reason why. Bacteria are on everyone's skin and under fingernails. Healthy skin provides a barrier that keeps the bacteria out so they can't harm the body. But kids with AD sometimes scratch open their skin, giving bacteria a way to get into the body and cause an infection.

Infections in other parts of the body can also trigger your skin to flare. A cold, flu, fever blister, or athlete's foot fungus puts stress on your body. Your skin may flare from this stress.

Why Should I Worry?

When your skin is infected it takes longer to heal. Infections also cause more itching as they heal. Unfortunately, even if you practice good skin care, infections are tough to prevent—most kids with AD get them every once in a while.

What Can I Do?

The good news is if you start to treat a skin infection early on, and take good care of your skin during the times you have a cold, flu, or other illness, you may be able to prevent flare-ups from getting worse.

Infected skin · Bacteria · Break in skin

What Should I Watch For?

If you notice any of the symptoms listed on the poster below, tell a parent. You should see your doctor immediately. He or she may give you an antibiotic ointment or pill to help you fight the infection. Be sure to follow your doctor's instructions for applying or taking any medication. Even if you're starting to feel better, it's important to continue to use your medicine to be sure that the infection is cured.

"Whenever I'm sick, my skin is very bad. Once my ankle became very infected from scratching and I got a blood infection. I had to go to the hospital and keep my ankle wrapped up and stay inside."

Rachel P.
Age 5, Florida

Signs of Infection

To keep your skin as healthy as possible, learn to recognize these signs of infection:
- Skin feels warm and more red or tender than usual.
- Skin may have bumps that ooze a yellowish fluid.
- Some infections can have an unpleasant odor.

List things you want to remember about infections, and your doctor's instructions for medications, on page 46.

Scratching Struggles

Sometimes even after you do all you can to avoid the things that make you itch, you still end up scratching. Is there anything else you can do?

Daytime Scratching

Many kids scratch the most when they're bored, or when their hands aren't busy doing other things. Often, people with AD don't even realize they're scratching! If this is true for you, try to keep busy by doing activities with other people, especially things that involve your hands. You can also protect your skin by wearing clothes that cover. Remember, the less you scratch, the less you'll itch!

"I play the piano when I itch. It helps me forget about my itchiness—and keeps my fingers busy!"

Sydney J.
Age 8, New Jersey

"I scratch when I watch TV—I do it with out thinking. Sometimes I put on pants so I can't scratch open my skin."

Michael L.
Age 11, Illinois

Give your hands something fun to do, such as playing cards or creating crafts.

Nighttime Advice

It's hard to feel perky in the morning when you've been up scratching all night. If your itching is keeping you from sleeping, try these suggestions to help soothe your skin:

- Cover the itchy area with a cold, wet washcloth for a while, then apply moisturizer. (For extra cool relief, try keeping your skin cream in the refrigerator.)

- Your doctor may prescribe an antihistamine, which will ease your itching and may make you sleepy.
- Cut your fingernails so they're as short as possible. Since even short nails can break open your skin, file them smooth so that if you scratch while you sleep, you'll do less damage. Lightweight cotton gloves (found in many drugstores) can keep your nails covered and skin safe.

Scratch-Stoppers

Sleep tight with these tips.

"When I was little, my mom would tell me a story about somewhere far away to relax me and help me forget about being itchy. If I'm having a bad night, I'll still go to my mom and ask for a story to take me away."

Tyler V.
Age 12, Illinois

"To keep from scratching open my skin while I sleep, I wear long socks and pajamas with long sleeves and pants. Because of all that clothing, my mom makes it cooler in my room at night."

Maxine M.
Age 6, Florida

"Sometimes I take an ice pack to bed. If I wake up in the middle of the night feeling itchy, I put the ice pack on my skin."

Jeffrey J.
Age 9, Michigan

Turn to page 46 to write thoughts you have about scratching.

"I have eczema on my fingers. Two of my nails even fell off, so sometimes I hide my hands. To make them look more presentable, I paint my nails and wear bracelets."

Suzy M.
Age 13, Illinois

* Check with your doctor before using nail polish.

"Sometimes when I have trouble with my homework, I start to scratch my arms. I usually take a break and put a cool washcloth on my neck. It actually helps my arms stop itching!"

Alexis S.
Age 8, California

"I used to get embarrassed when I had to wear shorts for basketball. But my coach is a doctor, so he knows about eczema. He told my teammates that's what I have, and that it's no big deal. I've been more relaxed since then."

Michael L.
Age 11, Illinois

"Windbreaker pants keep me from itching in wintertime. They're real loose and don't rub on my legs."

Chandon H.
Age 7, Florida

Remember: you're not alone! Here are some more thoughts —and solutions— from kids with AD.

"I wear plain shorts but bright-colored shirts with interesting details. That way, people will look up and not notice my legs as much."

Alyssa C.
Age 12, California

"When I get school pictures taken, I put foundation makeup around my mouth to cover up the flares."

John K.
Age 9, Illinois

* Check with your doctor before trying any type of makeup.

"I can't go to parties at carpeted houses because I'm allergic to dust mites. Sometimes friends have their party outdoors or roll up their rugs and put them away, so I can come over and not itch."

Nayha R.
Age 7, Massachusetts

"Don't let other people convince you to be embarrassed about your skin. I've always felt eczema was a part of me, and I think people see it doesn't bother me, so it doesn't bother them."

Tyler V.
Age 12, Illinois

The Emotional Side

Understanding your **feelings** and taking care of them is just as **important** as understanding and taking care of your skin problems. This section offers suggestions to **soothe** your emotions when they flare.

A Flood of Feelings

Having AD can bring out a wide range of feelings in you. The reactions described on these pages are all normal. In fact, you may have felt several of these emotions at the same time.

I feel **embarrassed** when my skin flares—I just want to hide.

I'm **confused** about what's happening with my skin.

I **worry** that my AD will get worse.

I get **angry**—it's not fair that I have to spend so much time taking care of my skin.

I **envy** other kids who have perfect skin.

I feel **guilty** because I scratch even though I know I shouldn't.

I'm **afraid** no one will want to be my friend.

I feel **alone**, like nobody understands what I'm going through.

I don't want to talk about it. There's **nothing wrong** with my skin!

Feeling Flawed

AD not only affects the outside of your body—it can also affect what goes on inside your mind. It's natural to feel upset sometimes. AD can be a frustrating disease—after all, you can't always control what it does to your skin. But you *can* try to keep it from controlling your emotions, too.

How can you gain power over your eczema? Talking about your embarrassment, anger, or worry can help. Sharing your feelings with a family member, doctor, or good friend lets you vent some of the emotions that upset you. And together you may be able to come up with some solutions for what's bothering you! (Pages 32-35 offer some tips for talking about AD.)

If your itching has gone on so long that you are overwhelmed by feelings of anger, hopelessness, or depression, tell a parent or some other adult you trust so you can get the help you need.

Accepting Reality

It may seem tough to accept the fact that your skin is not normal. Some kids with eczema won't admit they need to take special care of their skin. It's as if by pretending they don't have AD, they can make it go away. This is also a natural reaction. But if you feel this way and don't eventually change the behaviors that harm your skin, there's a good chance your condition will just get worse. Think you could use a little help improving your attitude? Turn the page!

Have a Healthy Attitude

You may be stuck with skin problems right now, but you don't have to be stuck with a bad attitude, too. Having a healthy outlook is the first step towards having healthier skin!

Don't Be So Hard on Yourself!

If you feel like the whole world is staring at your flares, it's time to do a reality check. Most people are more focused on the flaws they see in *themselves* than the flares you see on your skin. Instead of hiding from people, tell them about your AD. (Pages 32-33 can help you find the words to use.) Other people will probably accept the fact that your skin isn't perfect—and you should, too!

 "My mom says that everyone has something that they're embarrassed by or afraid of, so just be yourself. Sometimes my friends ask about my skin. When we talk, they remember that someone in their family has rashes, too."

Dominic P.
Age 9, Michigan

Don't Make Assumptions

Sometimes kids with AD think others are avoiding them because of their disease. Before you assume this is true, make sure you haven't withdrawn from others out of embarrassment or fear of what they might think. Other kids might mistake your nervousness as being unfriendly. Kids might also be staying away because they don't know what to say or how to act. They may need *you* to break the ice.

 "Try to be friendly. Before you know it, you'll start playing with others and they won't even notice your skin. They'll just like you."

Jeffrey J.
Age 9, Michigan

Remember: there's much more to you than your AD. The qualities you have—such as your friendliness, sense of humor, or talents— are what other people like and admire in you. Eczema is just a small part of who you are.

Take Risks

Has your skin ever kept you from trying out for something you might enjoy, like a school play or a sports team? Sometimes kids with eczema unknowingly use their disease as an excuse for not trying something. It's easier to blame their AD than to face their fear of trying something new.

If this is true for you, here's a tip: go for it! It may not be easy, but refuse to let AD keep you in hiding. As you interact with people, your self-esteem will increase, you'll focus less on your skin, and others will get the chance to know the real you—*and* see that you aren't held back by your skin. An added benefit: your skin might even improve since you may scratch less because your new activity will keep you so busy!

Tips for Talking

Wish others could understand what you're going through? Have a hard time putting into words how you feel? Don't know what to say when someone teases you? Here are some hints for handling the topic of AD.

What to Say

You may wonder what to say about your flares to friends or others who are curious. Try explaining it straight out. "It's kind of like an allergic reaction. My skin gets red and itchy, but it goes away after a while." Explaining AD lets others know they have nothing to be afraid of. And real friends will want to help you through rough times. It's not surprising—you'd be supportive of them, too, wouldn't you?

Teasing Troubles

Unfortunately, kids with AD are sometimes teased. What can you do if this happens? Some kids say that presenting a report about eczema in class helps. Talking openly about their disease shows they accept it and consider it an interesting and important subject. Once your classmates know the facts, they'll probably adopt your positive attitude, too.

Teacher Talk

Sometimes AD can interfere with school-work. A sleepless night of scratching might make it hard to pay attention in class the next day. A flare-up that's severe may even keep you home. If you miss a lot of school, you might have trouble keeping your grades up. What can you do?

You and your parents should meet with your teachers to discuss your AD. Teachers need to know that you may have trouble sitting still when your itching is at its worst. There may also be days a teacher needs to excuse you so that you can apply moisturizer or take medication.

Words of Wisdom

These kids don't let their eczema get them down. Read their advice for how to handle AD hassles.

 "I explain that eczema is a skin rash that doctors don't know the cure for, but kids can't catch it from me. If you are teased, you should just say, 'I am like this and you'll have to deal with it.'"

Amy R.
Age 11, Connecticut

 "Once I heard a boy's mom tell my teacher she didn't want her son to sit next to me because my skin sometimes cracks and bleeds. So my mom got a letter from my doctor that explains eczema. She gave copies to all the kids to take home. Now, the boy I told you about is my best buddy. He even goes with me to the school nurse when I'm itching and need medicine. "

Eric R.
Age 7, Connecticut

 "My friends like me because of what's on the inside of me. If your friends don't like you because of what you look like, they're not true friends."

Sharita R.
Age 11, Virginia

 "Some kids at school are very caring and concerned. They help me when my eczema hurts me too much to do things."

Christopher D.
Age 8, Florida

Your Treatment Team

When you're up against AD, you need supportive teammates. Your doctor and family members are important players on your side. Here's a game plan for keeping communication open and effective.

If you have questions about your skin or treatment at home, write them down in your Skin Profile on pages 44-46 and bring them to your next doctor's appointment.

Doc Discussions

You and your doctor are working together to keep your eczema under control. Be open and honest when talking about your skin. The more information you can give to the doctor, the better. If you've let your treatment slide, tell the truth—your doctor needs to know all the facts to care for your skin the best way he or she can.

It's also important that you understand your treatment plan and follow it carefully. If you're confused by or disappointed with some part of your therapy, talk with your doctor. Don't be afraid to ask questions. Your doctor will be glad you're interested and want to help you learn more about your skin.

"My doctor really understands how I feel. She treats me like a grownup and works hard to make me feel better. The office is even starting a support group for kids with AD."

Tyler V.

Age 12, Illinois

Family Matters!

Your eczema may sometimes lead to family arguments. If your itching is keeping you and other family members up at night, everyone may be moody. Family support is very important for anyone who has eczema, so here are a few things you can do to help everyone keep their cool when tempers heat up:

- If you feel your parents are hounding you about your treatment, realize that they're just trying to keep you comfortable by preventing your AD from flaring. Do your part to take care of your skin so your parents don't feel they must constantly remind you.

- Like you, your parents may feel frustrated. It's hard for them to watch someone they love struggle with eczema. Talk with your parents about your feelings. This will help all of you deal with problems you may be having.

"It helps to talk to my mom because she has AD, too. I got the gene from her."

Delynn S.
Age 11, Georgia

"My mom says it's what's on the inside that makes me the person I am, not my skin. My skin is just more red than other kids', and there's nothing wrong with that."

Danielle B.

- It's natural for you to feel envious of sisters or brothers who don't have skin problems. A sibling might also get upset with you or your parents if they spend extra time helping you take care of your skin. Try reading this book—or parts of it—with your siblings. Doing something fun together can also strengthen your relationship.

Create a Flare Calendar

You can use a calendar like this to help you discover what may be causing your skin to flare. Each week, jot down new or unusual things you do such as your first soccer practice or trying new foods. Also record any situations that make you emotional, such as a fight with a friend or a big test. Whenever you notice a flare, write that down, too ("F"). Can you connect your flares to any of the events or situations you experienced? Talk with a parent about how you can avoid or better handle situations in the future that cause you to flare. Visit **www.fujisawa.com** to print calendars or use your own.

January
(month)

Sunday	Monday	Tuesday	Wednesday	Thursday	Friday	Saturday
	1 New Year's Day	**2** School Starts F	**3** F	**4** F	**5** F	**6**
7	**8**	**9**	**10**	**11**	**12** Mom's birthday, ate chocolate cake	**13**
14	**15** no school, went sledding	**16**	**17** Jack's birthday, drank fruit punch	**18**	**19**	**20**
21 spaghetti dinner F	**22** F	**23** F	**24** F	**25** Sheila's birthday, went ice skating	**26**	**27**
28	**29**	**30** class field trip to museum	**31**			

The Healing Side

It may often seem like you have no **control** over your AD.
When it comes to **caring** for your skin, however, *you're* in charge!
This section contains tips for **moisturizing**, information about
medicating, and a helpful skin **profile** for you to fill out.

Flare Care

Taking time *every* day to moisturize may seem like a drag—especially during those periods when your skin is doing better. Here are some tips to make your skin treatment more tolerable.

Set Up a Center

Turn an area of your bathroom or bedroom into a skin-care center. Keep moisturizers and medicines handy. Hang inspirational posters to keep you motivated. Photos of yourself when you're looking your best might inspire you to stick to your treatment. Every time you do your skin care, try to relax by focusing on positive things.

"I think of skin care as a way of recharging my energy. I get tired of itching and sore from scratching. Putting on moisturizer or medication helps me get through the day more comfortably."

John~Franklin D.
Age 13, Illinois

Stay in Supply

Keep moisturizers available everywhere you might need them.

"I keep lip balm and Vaseline in my back pack, in my desk at school, in both of our cars, and in our boat so I can put them on whenever I need to. "

John K.
Age 9, Illinois

Have a Routine

Make skin care part of your daily routine along with other activities such as brushing your teeth. If you moisturize at the same time every day, you'll be less likely to miss a treatment. And don't be tempted to take days off when your AD improves, or your itching and rash just might start all over again!

"Stick to a routine. If you do the same thing day after day, it just becomes a part of you."

Tyler V.
Age 12, Illinois

"I wrote 'skin treatment' on a piece of paper and taped it on my bedroom wall where I see it every day. That helps me remember to do my treatment in the morning and night, and during the day whenever my skin is feeling dry."

Nicole P.
Age 13, California

Make It Amusing

Play games while you moisturize, on your own or with your family.

■ Dab your cream or ointment on in a pattern, then connect the dots. You can also play tic-tac-toe using your moisturizer as markers.

■ Smooth your moisturizer on in a thick layer, then draw pictures on your "easel." Erase by gently rubbing the moisturizer into your skin.

"I make polka-dots with my moisturizer all over, then I rub it in. It looks funny when I look in the mirror and it's less boring that way."

Alyssa C.
Age 12, California

Take Extra Care

Remember to be doubly devoted to your skin at stressful times. Apply more moisturizer than usual, don't miss a treatment, and be sure to keep any open scratches clean.

"My mom makes sure she washes her hands before she puts moisturizer on me."

Danielle B.

Turn to page 47 to come up with your own daily routine schedule.

Therapy and Side Effects

Here are some of the most common types of therapy. Your doctor may prescribe a few, several, or all of the treatments listed on these pages, depending on what he or she thinks will be best for you.

Moisturizers

Creams and ointments applied to the skin keep it from drying out, which helps prevent flares and infections. Moisturizers also keep your skin softer and more flexible so it doesn't break open as easily.

Moisturizing can be time-consuming and may leave you feeling greasy or as if your skin can't breathe.

"If your skin hurts, don't rub your moisturizer in—tap it on instead."

Eric R.
Age 7, Connecticut

Steroids

Although steroid creams and ointments don't cure AD, they *can* calm itchy, swollen, red skin. Your doctor will give you the mildest steroid possible to avoid side effects.

If not used properly, steroids can cause discoloration or skin thinning, so listen very carefully when your doctor tells you how to use them (how, when, and how long to apply). Be sure to wash your hands after applying steroids and other medications.

Antihistamines

These are pills or liquid medicines that help stop itching

Some antihistamines may make you sleepy, which is helpful if your AD is keeping you up at night but may be a problem if you're trying to pay attention in school. Antihistamines can also have the *opposite* effect—they may cause you to feel restless or fidgety.

"If my skin itches, I flick it, blow on it, do whatever I have to do—I just don't scratch it!"

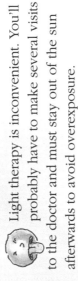

Jeffery J.
Age 9, Michigan

Antibiotics

These can be pills, liquid medicine, or creams and ointments that cut down on the amount of bacteria on skin. If bacteria are reduced, flares may be, too.

If you use or take antibiotics too often, or for too long a time, the bacteria will eventually become so strong the medicine won't work anymore.

Light Therapy

Special lights, sometimes combined with a medicine you swallow, can help calm your skin. This treatment may be used to give people a break from steroids.

Light therapy is inconvenient. You'll probably have to make several visits to the doctor and must stay out of the sun afterwards to avoid overexposure.

New Therapies

There are many new medicines being developed. Some are applied to the skin and relieve itching, redness, and swelling. Unlike steroids, you may be able to use some of these new drugs on your face as needed.

When first applied, some of these medicines may sting slightly, increase itching, or make your skin sensitive to heat. After several applications, however, the discomfort usually fades.

"I've been trying lots of different medicines, hoping to find one that works. It took a long time, but we finally found one that helps my skin."

Alexis S.
Age 8, California

Looking Ahead

You've learned things you can do to help your skin *now*—read on to find out what the future may hold. Plus, learn how you can help other kids the way the kids in this book helped you.

Will I Ever Be AD-Free?

Doctors can't predict how long you may struggle with AD. Most kids grow out of this disease by their early teen years. But a small percentage of people continue to have problems with eczema as adults. While this might not seem like great news, it may help you to know that *remissions*—periods of time when the disease goes away—are common. Remissions can last for months or even years, and often happen as the result of good skin care.

Life after AD

If you are lucky enough to grow out of eczema, you may still have a few related health concerns: hay fever and asthma are very common in people who have AD. These are allergic reactions just like atopic dermatitis is. More than half of all kids with eczema either already have hay fever or asthma or develop one or both in the future.

You'll also still have to take good care of your skin. People with AD in their past will usually experience one or more of the following skin challenges in their future:
- dry skin that's easily irritated
- hand eczema
- skin infections.

You've learned the techniques of good skin care—stick with them, and they'll help you reduce future skin problems!

There's a good chance you'll grow out of AD, but some kids continue to experience problems with the disease into adulthood.

Share Your Experience

Remember, millions of kids are dealing with atopic dermatitis. You met just a few in this book. If you'd like to meet more—or share your own tips, thoughts, or experiences—visit **www.fujisawa.com** or write to the address below. We'll post as many comments as we can on this web site so that other kids can learn from your experience. Let us hear from you!

Fujisawa Healthcare, Inc.
Medical Information Dept.
Three Parkway North Center
Deerfield, IL 60015-2548

Here is a place for you to write down questions for your doctor and keep notes about all the things that affect your skin—both good and bad. You might want to take these pages with you when you visit your doctor, to record product names or the doctor's instructions for treatment. Your doctor may also find it helpful to see the notes you keep on your skin.

My Skin Profile

Bathing

These are questions I have for my doctor about bathing:_____

_____

These are my doctor's instructions for bathing (how long? how often? skin cleansers and

shampoos to try): _____

_____

_____

These are the bath products that work best for me: _____

_____

Moisturizing

These are questions I have for my doctor about moisturizing:_____

_____

These are my doctor's suggestions for moisturizing (products to try, instructions for applying):

_____

These are the moisturizers that work best for me: _____

Irritants

These are questions I have for my doctor about irritants: _____
_____

These are the things I try to avoid because they irritate my skin: _____
_____

Allergens

These are questions I have for my doctor about allergens: _____
_____

These are the things I am allergic to: _____
_____

Here is how I deal with these allergens to keep them from aggravating my skin: _____
_____
_____

Weather

These are questions I have for my doctor about how weather affects my skin: _____
_____

This kind of weather is the worst for my skin (hot/cold/dry/humid): _____
_____

Here is what I do to help my skin during this season: _____
_____

Stress

These are questions I have for my doctor about stress: _____

_____

These are some situations or times when I feel upset or stressed: _____

_____

Here are suggestions my family, friends, or doctor gave me to help me deal with my stress:

_____

_____

Medications

These are questions I have for my doctor about infections and/or my medications:_____

_____

These are my doctor's instructions for treating my infection and/or for using medications:

_____

_____

Scratching

These are questions I have for my doctor about scratching:_____

_____

These are the times I tend to scratch most often:_____

Here are my ideas to keep busy so I won't scratch:_____

_____

My Daily Routine

Your skin will stay healthiest when you stick to a regular skin-care routine. Here's a sample list of activities you might do every day. Ask your doctor or parent to help you create your own daily routine to follow. Write out your schedule below, then keep it handy so you can follow it each day. Your can print more daily routine pages at **www.fujisawa.com**.

Time	Skin Care	Time	Skin Care
6:00 am	wake up, shower, apply moisturizer, take medicine		
7:00 am	eat good breakfast		
3:00 pm	soccer practice		
4:30 pm	shower, moisturize		
7:00 pm	homework (start studying for test, work on report)		
8:00 pm	get clothes ready for school tomorrow		
8:15 pm	moisturize, take medicine		
8:45 pm	get ready for bed, read a book to relax		

"I always remember what my mom told me: that I shouldn't compare myself to other children. I also tell myself that I should be proud of who I am—proud of myself and my accomplishments."

Nicole P.
Age 13, California

"If I didn't have eczema, I might have been one of those people who judged others by their appearance. Eczema has probably made me a better person."

Heather M.
Age 13, Connecticut

"Whenever I get really upset and ask, 'Why me?' my mom points out that there are other people sicker than me. I remember that I'm lucky to be able to run and play."

Christopher D.
Age 9, Florida

"AD has made me think about how kids feel when they're different—like if they're a different race, or whatever. I try to treat everyone in my school the same. We're all equals, and everyone has feelings."

Tyler V.
Age 12, Illinois

Think nothing good can come out of AD? Here's how it changed the way these kids look at themselves—*and* others!

"To keep myself from scratching I go rollerblading a lot. All that practice helped me become a much better skater!"

Sharita R.
Age 11, Virginia

"My sister and I both have AD. I help by reminding her not to scratch and by listening to her when other kids make her feel bad. At least we're going through it together."

Charlotte M.
Age 8, Florida

"Your eczema might improve as you get older. Mine has, and now I'm not as embarrassed about it."

Amy R.
Age 11, Connecticut

"When I feel sad, my brothers remind me that everyone is different. And like I always say: eczema is a tough thing to deal with, but I'm *way* tougher than this disease!"

Eric R.
Age 8, Connecticut